To give the Bible its rightful place
is to bring glory to God,
health to the church
and light to the world.

JOHN R.W. STOTT

GOD'S BOOK FOR GOD'S PEOPLE

InterVarsity Press
Downers Grove
Illinois 60515

Published in the United States of America by InterVarsity Press, Downers Grove, Illinois, with permission from Universities and Colleges Christian Fellowship, Leicester, England.

InterVarsity Press is the book-publishing division of Inter-Varsity Christian Fellowship, a student movement active on campus at hundreds of universities, colleges and schools of nursing. For information about local and regional activities, write IVCF, 233 Langdon St., Madison, WI 53703.

Distributed in Canada through InterVarsity Press, 860 Denison St., Unit 3, Markham, Ontario L3R 4H1, Canada.

Scripture quotations are from the Revised Standard Version of the Bible, copyrighted 1946, 1952, © 1971, 1973.

Cover photograph: Jim Whitmer

ISBN 0-87784-396-1

Printed in the United States of America

Library of Congress Cataloging in Publication Data

Stott, John R. W.
    God's book for God's people.

    1. Bible—Evidences, authority, etc.   2. Bible—
Inspiration.   I. Title.
BS480.S73   1983   220.1'3   82-21203
ISBN 0-87784-396-1

---

15   14   13   12   11   10   9   8   7   6   5   4   3   2   1
95   94   93   92   91   90   89   88   87   86   85   84   83

1 God & the Bible *11*
The Reasonableness of Revelation *12*
The Way of Revelation *14*
The Purpose of Revelation *21*
Conclusion *22*

2 Christ & the Bible *25*
The Scriptures Bear Witness to Christ *26*
Christ Bears Witness to the Scriptures *31*
Conclusion *37*

3 The Holy Spirit & the Bible *41*
The Searching Spirit *45*
The Revealing Spirit *48*
The Inspiring Spirit *49*
The Enlightening Spirit *53*
Conclusion *58*

4 The Church & the Bible *61*
The Church Needs the Bible *64*
The Church Serves the Bible *70*
Conclusion *72*

5 The Christian & the Bible *75*
Revelations of God *80*
Promises of Salvation *81*
Commandments to Obey *84*
Conclusion *88*

Postscript *91*

65723

Preface

The substance of this little book was given as a series of five sermons in All Souls Church, Langham Place, London, during February and March 1980. I am grateful to Michael Baughen, rector of All Souls, for inviting me to preach them; to Inter-Varsity Press (UK) for suggesting that they should be written up for publication; to Mark Labberton, my former study assistant, for working through the first draft and making a number of helpful suggestions; and to Vivienne Curry for typing the final draft.

Although I have striven to eliminate the more ob-vious sermonic touches and have elaborated some points which (owing to the constraints of the pulpit) were skimpy, the material remains substantially what it was when first delivered. The book's origin as sermons explains some of its characteristics. Each chapter seeks to expound a biblical text. There are no footnotes. The style is colloquial rather than literary. And the readership I have had in mind is similar to the composition of the All Souls church family, namely, students and other thoughtful lay people who want to think seriously about the authority and relevance of the Bible.

The book claims to be no more than introductory. Important questions which are being discussed in scholarly circles today—questions, for example, about the meaning of language, the influence of culture, the sociology of knowledge and the perception of truth—are hardly raised here. This is a basic book about the historic Christian attitude to Scripture and about the Bible's own understanding of itself, both of which need to be restated in every generation and which remain the essential perspective from which to grapple with other pressing problems.

Introduction

I imagine we all know that the Bible continues to be a world best seller. I am told that the *Qur'an* (Koran) has now been translated into 128 languages. But the whole Bible has been translated into 275 languages, the New Testament into 495 more and at least one book of the Bible into 940 more. This makes a total of 1,710 languages and dialects into which some major portion of the Bible has been translated. In 1979 the United Bible Societies distributed 501 million copies of the Bible, and the total world sales by all publishers must run into thousands of millions. Why? Why does this old book remain at the top of the list?

Paradoxically, however, this much purchased book is a much neglected book. Probably tens of thousands of people who buy the Bible never read it. Even in churches, knowledge of the Bible is abysmal. Thirty years ago Cyril Garbett, then Archbishop of York, wrote that "the majority of men and women [in England] neither say their prayers, except in some terrifying emergency, nor read their Bibles, unless to look for help in a crossword puzzle, nor enter a church from one end of the year to the other, except for a baptism, a marriage and a funeral." And if that was true thirty years ago, it is even more true today. Few parents read the Bible to their children, let alone teach them out of it. Few church members make a practice of daily Bible meditation. Few preachers wrestle conscientiously with the biblical text so as to grasp both its original meaning and its contemporary application. And some church leaders are brash enough publicly to express their disagreement with its plain doctrinal or ethical teaching. It is a tragic situation. What can be done to remedy it?

I am convinced that the Bible is a book, indeed *the* book, for today. A recognition of its unique inspiration and consequent authority has until quite recently been part of the historic faith of all Christian churches. Certainly submission to the authority of Scripture, or, as I think we should express it better, submission to the authority of God as it is mediated to us through Scripture, has always been and still remains a major hallmark of evangelical Christians. We believe its instruction. We embrace its promises. We seek to obey its commands. Why so? Mainly because we believe the Bible is the Word of *God,* but also because he speaks to us through it with a living voice.

The Bible was the book for yesterday. Without doubt it will be the book for tomorrow. But for us it is the book for today. It is God's Word for today's world. Its continuing popularity, its regrettable neglect and its contemporary relevance are three good reasons why we should give our minds to the Bible, God's book for God's people.

1
God
& the
Bible

T HE TOPIC "GOD AND THE BIBLE" introduces us to the subject of revelation. In Isaiah 55:8-11, we hear God himself speaking:

My thoughts are not your thoughts,
   neither are your ways my ways, says the LORD.
For as the heavens are higher than the earth,
   so are my ways higher than your ways
   and my thoughts than your thoughts.
For as the rain and the snow come down from
      heaven,
   and return not thither but water the earth,
making it bring forth and sprout,

giving seed to the sower and bread to the eater,
so shall my word be that goes forth from my mouth;
it shall not return to me empty,
but it shall accomplish that which I purpose,
and prosper in the thing for which I sent it.

From this great text there are at least three important
lessons to learn.

The Reasonableness of Revelation

Some people find the very concept of revelation difficult. The idea that God should disclose himself to
mankind strains their credulity. "Why should he?"
they ask, "and how could he?" My response is that the
evident necessity of divine revelation makes the notion
eminently reasonable. Most people in every age have
felt baffled by the mysteries of human life and human experience. So most people have admitted that
they need wisdom from outside themselves if they are
ever to fathom the meaning of their own being, let
alone the meaning of the being of God, if indeed there
is a God. Let me go right back to Plato. He speaks in
the *Phaedo* about our having to sail the seas of darkness
and doubt on the little raft of our own understanding, "not without risk," he adds, "as I admit, if a man
cannot find some word of God which will more surely
and safely carry him."

Without revelation, without divine instruction and
direction, we human beings feel ourselves to be like a
boat drifting rudderless on the high seas, like a leaf
that is being tossed helplessly by the wind, like a blind

person groping in the darkness. How can we find our way? More important, how can we find *God's* way without his direction? The impossibility of human beings' discovering God by their own unaided intellect is very plainly aserted in Isaiah 55:8-9. "My thoughts are not your thoughts, neither are your ways my ways, says the LORD. For as the heavens are higher than the earth, so are my ways higher than your ways and my thoughts than your thoughts." In other words, there is a great gulf fixed between God's mind and human minds. The text expresses a contrast between the ways and the thoughts of God on the one hand, and the ways and the thoughts of human beings on the other. That is, between what we think and do, and what God thinks and does, there is this great chasm. The thoughts and ways of God are as much higher than the thoughts and ways of man as the heavens are higher than the earth: that means infinity.

Consider God's thoughts. How can we discover his thoughts or read his mind? Why, we can't even read each other's thoughts. We try to. We look into each other's faces to see if they are smiling or frowning. We peer into each other's eyes to see whether they are flashing or twinkling or somber or bright. But it is a risky business. If I were to stand in the pulpit silent and maintain a poker face, you would not have the foggiest notion what I was thinking about. Let's try it. Let me stop talking for a few moments. . . . Could you tell what was going on in my mind? Could you guess? No. I was mentally scaling the steeple of All Souls Church, trying to reach the top. But no one knew. No one could possibly have the faintest notion what I was thinking or imagining. No one can read my mind. If we are silent, it is impossible to read one another's minds.

How much less possible is it (if indeed there are degrees of impossibility) for us to penetrate into the thoughts of Almighty God? His mind is infinite. His thoughts tower above our thoughts as the heavens tower above the earth. It is ludicrous to suppose that we could ever penetrate into the mind of God. There is no ladder by which our little minds can climb to his infinite mind. There is no bridge that we can throw across the chasm of infinity. There is no way to reach or to fathom God.

It is only reasonable to say, therefore, that unless God takes the initiative to disclose what is in his mind, we shall never be able to find out. Unless God makes himself known to us, we can never know him, and all the world's altars—like the one Paul saw in Athens—will bear the tragic inscription "To an unknown god" (Acts 17:23).

This is the place to begin our study. It is the place of humility before the infinite God. It is also the place of wisdom, as we perceive the reasonableness of the idea of revelation.

The Way of Revelation

Granted that it is reasonable for God to reveal himself, how has he done so? He has revealed himself, in principle, in the same way that we reveal or disclose ourselves to one another, that is, by both works and words, by things we do and say.

Creative art has always been one of the chief means of human self-expression. We are conscious that there is something inside us which has to come out, and we struggle to bring it to birth. For some people the appropriate medium is music or poetry; for others it is one of the visual arts—drawing, painting or photography, pottery, sculpture, carving or architecture, dance or drama. It is interesting that of these artistic media pottery is the one most frequently used of God in Scripture, presumably because the potter was a well-known figure in the villages of Palestine. So God is said to have "formed" or "fashioned" the earth, and mankind to dwell upon it (Gen 2:7; Ps 8:3; Jer 32:17). Moreover, he himself is seen in his works. "The heavens are telling the glory of God," and "the whole earth is full of his glory" (Ps 19:1; Is 6:3). Or, as Paul writes near the beginning of Romans, "What can be known about God is plain to them [the Gentile world], because God has shown it to them. Ever since the creation of the world his invisible nature, namely, his eternal power and deity, has been clearly perceived in the things that have been made" (Rom 1:19-20).

In other words, just as human artists reveal themselves in their painting, sculpture or music, so the divine Artist has revealed himself in the beauty, balance, intricacy and order of his creation. From it we learn, therefore, something of his wisdom, power and faithfulness. This is usually referred to as *natural revelation* because it has been given in and through nature.

It is not to this that the Isaiah text refers, however, but rather to the second and more direct way in which we make ourselves known to one another and God has made himself known to us, namely, through *words*. Speech is the fullest and most flexible means of communication between two human beings. When I remained silent and straight-faced in the pulpit, I was inscrutable to you. No one could discover what was going on in my mind. But now the situation has changed. I am speaking again. You know what I am thinking because I am no longer silent. I am clothing the thoughts of my mind in the words of my mouth. My words are conveying to you the thoughts and images of my mind.

Speech, then, is the best means of communication, and speech is the main model used in the Bible to illustrate God's self-revelation. Notice our text, verses 10 and 11: "As the rain and the snow come down from heaven, and . . . water the earth, making it bring forth and sprout, giving seed to the sower and bread to the eater, so shall my word be." Notice the second reference to heaven and earth: it is because the heavens are higher than the earth that the rain comes down from heaven to water the earth. Notice also that the writer goes straight from the thoughts in the mind of God to the words in the mouth of God: "So shall my word be that goes forth from my mouth; it shall . . . accomplish that which I purpose, and prosper in the thing for which I sent it." The parallel is plain. As the heavens are higher than the earth, but the rain comes down from heaven to water the earth, so God's thoughts are higher than our thoughts, but they come down to us because his word goes forth from his mouth and thus conveys his thoughts to us. As the prophet had said earlier, "The mouth of the LORD has spoken" (Is 40:5). He was referring to one of his own oracles, but he described it as a message coming out of the mouth of God. Or, as Paul wrote to Timothy, "All scripture is God-breathed [the literal translation of *theopneustos*]" (2 Tim 3:16). That is, Scripture is God's Word, issuing from God's mouth.

Having made the affirmation which our text expresses, I want now to add a couple of qualifications in order to clarify our understanding of how God spoke his Word.

First, *God's Word* (now recorded in Scripture) *was closely related to his activity.* Put differently, he spoke to his people by deeds as well as words. He made himself known to Israel in their history, and so directed its development as to bring to the Israelites now his salvation, now his judgment. Thus, he rescued the people from their slavery in Egypt; he brought them safely across the desert and settled them in the promised land; he preserved their national identity through the period of the judges; he gave them kings to rule over them, despite the fact that their demand for a human king was in part a repudiation of his own king ship; his judgment fell upon them for their persistent disobedience when they were deported into Babylonian exile; and then he restored them to their own land and enabled them to rebuild their nationhood and their temple. Above all, for us sinners and for our salvation, he sent his eternal Son, Jesus Christ, to be born, to live and work, to suffer and die, to rise and to pour out the Holy Spirit. Through these deeds, first in the Old Testament story but supremely in Jesus Christ, God was actively and personally revealing himself.

For this reason it has been fashionable for some theologians to distinguish sharply between *personal revelation* (through God's deeds) and *propositional revelation* (through his words), and then to reject the latter in favor of the former. This polarization, however, is as unfortunate as it is unnecessary. There is no need for us to choose between these two media of revelation. God used them both. Moreover, they were closely related to one another. For God's words interpreted his deeds. He raised up the prophets to explain what he was doing to Israel, and he raised up the apostles to explain what he was doing through Christ. It is true that the process of divine self-revelation culminated in the person of Jesus. He was God's Word made flesh. He showed forth the glory of God. To have seen him was to have seen the Father (Jn 1:14, 18; 14:9). Nevertheless, this historical and personal revelation would not have benefited us unless, along with it, God had unfolded for us the significance of the person and work of his Son.

We must, then, avoid the trap of setting personal and propositional revelation over against each other as alternatives. It is more accurate to say that God has revealed himself in Christ and in the biblical witness to Christ. Neither is complete without the other.

Second, *God's Word has come to us through human words*. When God spoke, he didn't shout audibly out of a clear blue sky. No, he spoke through prophets in the Old Testament and through apostles in the New Testament. Moreover, these human agents of the revelation of God were real people. Divine inspiration was not a mechanical process which reduced the human authors of the Bible to machines, whether dictating machines or tape recorders. Divine inspiration was a personal process, in which the human authors of the Bible were usually in full possession of their faculties. We have only to read the Bible in order to see that this is so. The writers of narrative (and there is a great deal of historical narrative in the Bible, Old and New Testament alike) used historical records. Some are quoted in the Old Testament. Luke tells us at the beginning of his Gospel of his own painstaking historical researches. Also, all the biblical authors developed their own distinctive literary styles and theological emphases. Hence the rich diversity of Scripture. Nevertheless, through their varied approaches God himself was speaking.

This truth of the double authorship of the Bible, namely, that it is the Word of God *and* the word of men, or more strictly the Word of God *through* the

words of men, is the Bible's own account of itself. The
Old Testament law, for example, is sometimes called
"the law of Moses" and sometimes "the law of God" or
"the law of the LORD." In Hebrews 1:1 we read that
God spoke to the fathers through the prophets. In
2 Peter 1:21, however, we read that *men* spoke from
God as they were moved by the Holy Spirit. Thus God
spoke and men spoke. They spoke from him, and he
spoke through them. Both these affirmations are true.

Further, we must hold the two affirmations together. As in the incarnate Word (Jesus Christ), so in
the written Word (the Bible), the divine and human
elements combine and do not contradict one another.
This analogy, which was developed quite early in the
history of the church, is often criticized today. And
obviously it is not exact, since Jesus was a person
whereas the Bible is a book. Nevertheless, the analogy
remains helpful, provided that we remember its limitations. For example, we must never affirm the deity
of Jesus in such a way as to deny his humanity, nor affirm his humanity in such a way as to deny his deity.
So with the Bible. On the one hand, the Bible is the
Word of God. God spoke, deciding himself what he in
tended to say, yet not in such a way as to distort the
personality of the human authors. On the other hand,
the Bible is the word of men. Men spoke, using their
faculties freely, yet not in such a way as to distort the
truth of the divine message.

The double authorship of the Bible will affect the
way in which we read it. Because it is the word of men,

we shall study it like every other book—using our minds, investigating its words and syntax, its historical origins and its literary composition. But because it is also the Word of God, we shall study it like no other book—on our knees, humbly, crying to God for illumination and for the ministry of the Holy Spirit, without whom we can never understand his Word.

The Purpose of Revelation

We have considered *how* God spoke: now, *why* did he speak? The answer is not just to teach us, but to save us; not just to instruct us, but specifically to instruct us "for salvation" (2 Tim 3:15). The Bible has this severely practical purpose.

Returning to Isaiah 55, we see this emphasis in verses 10 and 11. The rain and the snow come down to us from heaven and do not return. They accomplish a purpose on earth. They water it. They cause it to bring forth or sprout. They make it fruitful. Just so, God's Word, issuing from his mouth and disclosing his mind, does not return to him empty. It accomplishes a purpose. Moreover, God's purpose in sending rain to the earth and his purpose in speaking his Word to human beings are similar. In both cases it is fruitfulness. His rain makes the earth fruitful; his Word makes human lives fruitful. It saves them, changing them into the likeness of Jesus Christ. Salvation is certainly the context. In verses 6 and 7 the prophet has spoken of God's mercy and pardon, and in verse 12 he will go on to speak of the joy and peace of God's redeemed people.

In fact, here lies the chief difference between God's revelation in creation (*natural* because given in nature, and *general* because given to all mankind) and his revelation in the Bible (*supernatural* because given by inspiration, and *special* because given to and through particular people). Through the created universe God reveals his glory, power and faithfulness, but not the way of salvation. If we want to learn his gracious plan to save sinners, it is to the Bible that we must turn. For it is there that he speaks to us of Christ.

Conclusion

From our text in Isaiah 55 we have learned three truths. First, divine revelation is not only reasonable but indispensable. Without it we could never know God. Second, divine revelation is through words. God spoke through human words and in doing so explained his deeds. Third, divine revelation is for salvation. It points us to Christ as Savior.

My conclusion is very simple. It is a call to humility. Nothing is more hostile to spiritual growth than arrogance, and nothing is more conducive to spiritual growth than humility. We need to humble ourselves before the infinite God, acknowledging the limitations of our human mind (that we could never find him by ourselves), and acknowledging our own sinfulness (that we could never reach him by ourselves).

Jesus called this the humility of a little child. God hides himself from the wise and clever, he said, but reveals himself to "babes" (Mt 11:25). He was not denigrating our minds, for God has given them to us. Rather he was indicating how we are to use them. The true function of the mind is not to stand in judgment on God's Word but to sit in humility under it, eager to hear it, grasp it, apply it and obey it in the practicalities of daily living.

The humility of children is seen not only in the way they learn but also in the way they receive. Children are dependents. None of their possessions has been earned. All they have has been given to them freely. Like children, then, we are to "receive the kingdom of God" (Mk 10:15). Sinners do not deserve and cannot earn eternal life, which is the life of God's kingdom; we have to humble ourselves to receive it as the free gift of God.

2
Christ & the Bible

In CHAPTER ONE, "GOD AND the Bible," we considered the origin of Scripture, where it came from—the great subject of revelation. Now we shall be thinking not of its origin but of its purpose; we are asking not where has it come from, but for what has it been given?

Our text is John 5:39-40. Jesus, speaking to his Jewish contemporaries, says, "You search the scriptures, because you think that in them you have eternal life; and it is they that bear witness to me; yet you refuse to come to me that you may have life."

From these words of Jesus we learn two profound

and complementary truths about Christ and the Bible.

The Scriptures Bear Witness to Christ
Jesus himself says very plainly, "It is they that bear witness to me" (v. 39). The major function of Scripture is to bear witness to Christ.

Now the context in which this text is embedded is concerned with testimony to Christ. What testimony can validate the claims of Jesus of Nazareth? He himself tells us. To begin with, he does not rely on his own testimony to himself, as is clear from verse 31: "If I bear witness to myself, my testimony is not true." Jesus is not suggesting, of course, that he is telling lies about himself. Indeed he later rebuts a criticism of the Pharisees by insisting that his testimony to himself *is* true (8:14). His point here is that self-testimony is inadequate; there would be something suspicious about it if the only testimony he had came from him alone. No, "there is another who bears witness to me," he says (v. 32).

So the testimony he relies upon is not his own testimony. Nor is it human testimony, even the testimony of that outstanding witness John the Baptist. "You sent to John, and he has borne witness to the truth. Not that the testimony which I receive is from man" (vv. 33-34). So then, says Jesus, it isn't from me and it isn't from human beings. Of course, John was "a burning and shining lamp"(v. 35), and people had been willing "to rejoice for a while in his light." But the testimony that Jesus claimed was greater. It was greater than his own testimony to himself, and greater than the testimony of any human being, even of John. It was the testimony of his Father. "The Father who sent me has himself borne witness to me" (v. 37). Moreover, the Father's testimony to the Son took two forms. First, it was given through the mighty works, the miracles, which the Father enabled him to do (v. 36). But second, and more directly still, it was given through the Scriptures, which are the Father's testimony to the Son. Verses 36-39 make this plain:

> The testimony which I have is greater than that of John; for the works which the Father has granted me to accomplish, these very works which I am doing, bear me witness that the Father has sent me. And the Father who sent me has himself borne witness to me. His voice you have never heard, his form you have never seen; and you do not have his word abiding in you, for you do not believe him whom he has sent. You search the scriptures, because you think that in them you have eternal life; and it is they that bear witness to me.

It was the consistent teaching of Jesus that Old Testament Scripture was God's Word bearing witness to him. He said, for example, "Abraham rejoiced . . . to see my day" (Jn 8:56). Or here in John 5:46 he says, "Moses . . . wrote of me." Again, "the scriptures . . . bear witness to me" (v. 39). At the beginning of his ministry, when he went to worship in the synagogue at Nazareth, he read from Isaiah 61 about the Messiah's mission and message of liberation, and he added: "Today this scripture has been fulfilled in your hearing" (Lk 4:21). In other words, "If you want to know whom the prophet was writing about, he was writing about me." Jesus continued to say this kind of thing throughout his ministry. Even after the resurrection he had not changed his mind, for "he interpreted to them in all the scriptures the things concerning himself" (Lk 24:27). Thus from the beginning to the end of his ministry Jesus declared that the whole prophetic testimony of the Old Testament, in all its rich diversity, converged upon him: "The scriptures . . . bear witness to me."

But Jesus' Jewish contemporaries missed this testimony. They were very diligent students of the Old Testament, and we have no quarrel with them over their study. "You search the scriptures," Jesus said. They did. They spent hours and hours in the most meticulous examination of the minutiae of Old Testament Scripture. They used to count the number of words, even the number of letters, in every book of the Bible. They knew they had been entrusted with the oracles of God (Rom 3:2). They somehow thought that an accumulation of detailed biblical knowledge would bring them into right relationship with God. "You search the scriptures, because you think that in them you have eternal life." What an anomalous thing that was, to imagine that the Scriptures themselves could give eternal life! The Scriptures point to Christ as the Lifegiver and urge their readers to go to *him* for life. But instead of going to Christ to find life, they imagined that they could find life in Scripture itself. It is somewhat like getting a prescription from the doctor and then swallowing the prescription instead of getting and taking the medicine.

Some of us make the same mistake. We have an almost superstitious attitude to Bible reading, as if it had some magical efficacy. But there is no magic in the Bible or in the mechanical reading of the Bible. No, the written Word points to the Living Word and says to us, "Go to Jesus." If we do not go to the Jesus to whom it points, we miss the whole purpose of Bible reading.

Evangelical Christians are not, or ought not to be, what we are sometimes accused of being, namely, "bibliolaters," worshipers of the Bible. We do not worship the Bible; we worship the Christ of the Bible. Here is a young man who is in love. He has a girlfriend who has captured his heart. Or indeed she may be his fiancée, or his wife, and he is deeply in love with her. As a result he carries a photograph of his beloved in his wallet because it reminds him of her when she is far away. Sometimes, when nobody is looking, he might even take the photograph out and give it a surreptitious kiss. But kissing the photograph is a poor substitute for the real thing. And so it is with the Bible. We love it only because we love him of whom it speaks.

This is the main key to the understanding of Scripture. The Bible is God's picture of Jesus. It bears witness to him. So whenever we are reading the Bible, we must look for Christ. For example, the Old Testament Law is our "schoolmaster" to bring us to Christ (Gal

3:24 KJV). Because it condemns us for our disobedience, it makes Christ indispensable to us. It drives us
to him through whom alone we may find forgiveness.

Next, the Old Testament sacrifices foreshadow
that perfect sacrifice for sin made once and for all
upon the cross, the sacrifice of Christ for our redemp-
tion. Another example is the teaching of the Old Testament prophets who foretell the coming of the Messiah. They speak of him as the king of David's line during whose kingdom there will be peace, righteousness
and stability. They write of him as the "seed of Abraham" through whom all the nations of the world will
be blessed. They depict him as the "suffering servant
of the Lord" who will die for the sins of his people, and
as "the son of man coming in the clouds of heaven,"
whom all peoples will serve. All this rich imagery of
Old Testament prophecy bears witness to Christ.

When we move into the New Testament, Jesus
Christ comes yet more clearly into focus. The Gospels
are full of him. They speak of his birth and his public
ministry, of his words and works, of his death and
resurrection, and of his ascension and gift of the Holy
Spirit. The book of Acts tells us what Jesus continued
to do and teach through the apostles whom he had
chosen and commissioned. The letters of the apostles
set forth the glory of Jesus in his divine-human person and his saving work. When we come to the last
book of the Bible, the Revelation, it too is full of Christ.
For there we see him patrolling the churches on earth,
sharing God's throne in heaven, riding forth on a white

horse conquering, and coming in power and glory.

The old writers used to say that, just as in England every footpath and every country lane, linking on to others, will ultimately lead you to London, so every verse and every paragraph in the Bible, linking on to others, will ultimately lead you to Christ. The Scriptures bear witness to him. That is the first truth which is very plainly taught in our text.

Christ Bears Witness to the Scriptures

In declaring that the Scriptures bear witness to him, Jesus is himself bearing witness to them. When he spoke of the testimony of John the Baptist, he referred to it as human testimony (Jn 5:33-34) and added that the testimony which attested him was "not...from man." The testimony he had was greater. It was his Father's testimony through his works (v. 36) and his word (v. 38). Here then is Jesus' plain statement that the Old Testament Scriptures are his Father's "word," and that this biblical testimony was not human but divine.

This too was Jesus' consistent teaching. In fact, the major reason why we desire to submit to the authority of the Bible is that Jesus Christ authenticated it as possessing the authority of God. If we are to understand this point (as understand it we must), then we need to distinguish between the Old and the New Testaments. The Bible, of course, comprises them both; but Jesus was born and lived and died in the middle, between them. As a consequence, the way in which he authenticated the one is different from the way in which he authenticated the other. He looked back to the Old Testament, he looked on to the New Testament, but he authenticated them both.

1. Jesus endorsed the Old Testament. He not only described it as his Father's "word" and "witness," as we have seen; he also said that "scripture cannot be broken" (Jn 10:35). At the beginning of the Sermon on the Mount he declared, "Think not that I have come to abolish the law and the prophets; I have come not to abolish them but to fulfill them. For truly, I say to you, till heaven and earth pass away, not an iota, not a dot, will pass from the law until all is accomplished" (Mt 5:17-18).

Jesus' personal attitude toward the Old Testament Scriptures was one of reverent submission, for he believed that in submitting to the written Word he was submitting to his Father's Word. Since he believed in its divine origin, he interpreted his own messianic mission in the light of its prophetic testimony and added that certain things *must* come to pass because the Scripture *must* be fulfilled. Further, Jesus obeyed the moral injunctions of the Old Testament, so that in the temptations in the Judean wilderness he commanded the devil to leave him because of what stood written in Scripture. However subtle Satan's insinuations might be, Jesus was prepared neither to listen nor to negotiate. He was determined to obey God, not the devil, and what stood written in Scripture settled the issue for him (for example, Lk 4:4, 8, 12).

Jesus also made the Scripture his ground of appeal

in all his arguments with the religious leaders of his day. He was often engaged in controversy, and on every occasion it was to the Scriptures that he appealed. He criticized the Pharisees for adding their traditions to the Scriptures; he criticized the Sadducees for subtracting the supernatural (the resurrection) from the Scriptures. Thus Jesus exalted Scripture as his Father's Word which was to be both believed and obeyed. He permitted no deviation from it, either by addition or by subtraction.

Jesus declared, of course, that with him the time of fulfillment had come (see Mk 1:14-15) and that therefore the era of anticipation was over. This meant, as his followers soon recognized, that Gentiles were to be admitted to God's kingdom on equal terms with Jews, and that the Jewish ceremonial system had been rendered obsolete, including its dietary laws (Mk 7:19) and above all its blood sacrifices. But there is no example in the Gospels of Jesus' disagreeing with the doctrinal or ethical teaching of the Old Testament. On the contrary, he endorsed it. What he contradicted was the scribal misinterpretations and distortions of the Old Testament. This was his point in the Sermon on the Mount, in which six times he said in effect, "You have heard this, but I tell you something different." What they had heard were the so-called traditions of the elders. It was these which he was criticizing; it was not the teaching of Moses in the law. For what stood written in Scripture he received as his Father's Word.

If this is so, and the evidence is overwhelming, we

have to add that the disciple is not above his teacher.
It is inconceivable that a Christian who looks to Jesus
as his Teacher and Lord should have a lower view
of the Old Testament than he did. What is the sense in
calling Jesus "Teacher" and "Lord," and then disagreeing with him? We have no liberty to disagree
with him. His view of Scripture must become ours.
Since he believed Scripture, so must we. Since he
obeyed Scripture, so must we. He emphatically endorsed its authority.

**2. Jesus made provision for the writing of the New Tes-
tament.**   Just as God called the prophets in the Old
Testament to record and interpret what he was doing,
and then sent them to teach the children of Israel, so
Jesus called the apostles to record and interpret what
he was doing and saying, and then sent them to teach
the church and, indeed, the world. This is the meaning of the word *apostolos,* a person "sent" on a mission
with a message.

This parallel between the Old Testament prophets
and the New Testament apostles was deliberate. Jesus
chose twelve in order that they might be with him—to
hear his words, see his works and then bear witness out
of what they had seen and heard (compare Mk 3:14;
Jn 15:27). Next he promised them the Holy Spirit in
order to remind them of his teaching and to supple-
ment it, leading them into all the truth (Jn 14:25-26;
16:12-13). This explains why Jesus could then say to
the apostles, "He who listens to you listens to me; he
who receives you receives me; he who rejects you re-

jects me" (see Mt 10:40; Lk 10:16; Jn 13:20). In other words, he invested them with his authority so that people's attitude to their teaching would mirror their attitude to his. Later Jesus added Paul and maybe one or two others to the apostolic band, investing them with the same apostolic authority.

The apostles themselves recognized the unique authority they had been given as the teachers of the church. They did not hesitate on occasion to put themselves on a par with the Old Testament prophets, since they too were bearers of the Word of God (1 Thess 2:13). They spoke and wrote in the name and with the authority of Jesus Christ. They issued commandments and expected obedience (for example, 2 Thess 3). They even gave instructions that their letters should be read in the public assembly when Christians were gathered together for worship, thus placing them alongside the Old Testament Scriptures (see Col 4:16; 1 Thess 5:27). This is the origin of the practice, which continues to this day, of having an Old Testament and a New Testament lesson read in church.

A striking example of Paul's self-conscious apostolic authority occurs in his letter to the Galatians. He had climbed over the Taurus mountains on to the Galatian plateau to visit them, and he had arrived a sick man. He mentions some disfigurement, which had perhaps affected his eyesight (4:13-15), and goes on to say: "You did not scorn or despise me, but received me as an angel of God, as Christ Jesus" (v. 14). Not only had they welcomed him as God's "angel," or messenger, but they had actually listened to him as if he were Jesus Christ himself. Notice that he does not rebuke them for this. He does not say, "What on earth were you thinking about, that you should have given to me the deference that you would give to Christ?" No, he applauds them for the way they had treated him. It was not merely Christian courtesy which had motivated them to welcome a stranger. It was more than that. They had recognized him as a divine messenger, an apostle, who had come to them in the name and with the authority of Christ. So they had received him as if he were Christ.

Not only did the apostles understand the teaching authority they had been given, but the early church understood it also. As soon as all the apostles had died, church leaders knew that they had moved into a new postapostolic era. There was now no longer anybody in the church with the authority of a Paul or a Peter or a John. Bishop Ignatius of Antioch is perhaps the earliest clear example of this; he died about A.D. 110, which was very soon after John, the last surviving apostle, had died. On his way to Rome to be executed, Ignatius wrote a number of letters to the Ephesians, the Romans, the Trallians and others. Several times in these he wrote: "I do not, like Peter or Paul, issue you with commands. For I am not an apostle, but a condemned man." Now Ignatius was a bishop in the church. He is, in fact, one of the earliest witnesses to the rise of the episcopate. But, although he was a bishop, he knew he was not an apostle, and he therefore did not have an apostle's authority.

The early church clearly understood this difference. When the time came to fix the New Testament canon in the third century A.D., the test of canonicity was apostolicity. The essential questions to be asked of a disputed book were these: Had it been written by an apostle? If not, did it come from the circle of the apostles? Did it contain the teaching of the apostles? Did it have the imprimatur of the apostles? If in one of these ways it could be shown to be apostolic, then it was admitted into the canon of New Testament Scripture.

It is extremely important to recover today this understanding of the unique authority of Christ's apostles. For there are no apostles in the contemporary church. To be sure, there are missionaries and church leaders of different kinds who may be described as having an apostolic ministry. But there are no apostles like the Twelve and Paul who were eyewitnesses of the risen Lord (Acts 1:21-26; 1 Cor 9:1; 15:8-10) and who had received a special commission and inspiration from him. We have no right, therefore, to dismiss their teaching as if it were merely their own opinion. They were not speaking or writing in their own names, but in Christ's.

Conclusion

Let me sum up. We believe the Scriptures because of Christ. He endorsed the Old Testament, and he made provision for the writing of the New Testament by giving to the apostles his authority. We therefore receive the Bible from the hand of Jesus Christ. It is he who has invested it with his own authority. And since we are determined to submit to him, we are determined to submit to it. Our doctrine of Scripture is bound up with our loyalty to Jesus Christ. If he is our Teacher and our Lord, we have no liberty to disagree with him. Our view of Scripture must be his.

At this point some people raise an understandable objection. "The Scriptures bear witness to Christ and Christ bears witness to the Scriptures," they say, accurately summarizing what we have been saying. "But surely," they continue, "this reciprocal testimony, each bearing witness to the other, is a circular argument? Does it not assume the very truth you are wanting to prove? That is, in order to demonstrate the inspiration of Scripture you appeal to the teaching of Jesus, but you believe the teaching of Jesus only because of the inspired Scriptures. Isn't that a circular argument, and therefore invalid?" This is an important objection to face. But actually our argument has been misstated, for it is linear and not circular reasoning.

Let me put it in this way: When we first listen to the biblical witness to Christ, we read our New Testament with no preconceived doctrine of inspiration. We simply accept it as a collection of first-century historical documents, which indeed it is. Through this historical testimony, however, quite apart from any theory of biblical inspiration, the Holy Spirit brings us to faith in

Jesus. Then this Jesus, in whom we have come to believe, sends us back to the Bible and gives us in his teaching a doctrine of Scripture which we did not have when we started our reading. For he now tells us that its *historical* testimony is also *divine* testimony, and that through the human agency of prophets and apostles his Father is bearing witness to him.

Whenever you read the Bible, I want to beg you to remember its major purpose. Scripture is the Father's testimony to the Son. It points to him. It says to us, "Go to him in order to find life—abundant life—in him." Therefore any preoccupation with the biblical text which does not lead to a stronger commitment to Jesus Christ, in faith, love, worship and obedience, is seriously perverted. It brings us under the rebuke of Jesus. "You search the scriptures, because you think that in them you have eternal life; and it is they that bear witness to me; yet you refuse to come to me [to whom they bear witness] that you may have life."

Scripture, as Luther used to say, is the manger or cradle in which the infant Jesus lies. Don't let us inspect the cradle and forget to worship the Baby. Scripture, we might say, is the star which still leads wise people to Jesus. Don't let us allow our astronomical curiosity so to preoccupy us that we miss the house to which it is leading, and within it the Christ-child himself. Or, we might say, Scripture is the box in which the jewel of Jesus Christ is displayed. Don't let us admire the box and overlook the jewel.

Dr. Christopher Chavasse, formerly Bishop of

Rochester, once put the matter admirably. He said:
> The Bible is the portrait of our Lord Jesus Christ.
> The Gospels are the Figure itself in the portrait.
> The Old Testament is the background leading up
> to the divine Figure, pointing towards it and ab-
> solutely necessary to the composition as a whole.
> The Epistles serve as the dress and accoutrements
> of the Figure, explaining and describing it. Then
> while by our Bible reading we study the portrait as
> a great whole, the miracle happens, the Figure comes
> to life, and stepping down from the canvas of the
> written word the everlasting Christ of the Emmaus
> story becomes himself our Bible teacher, to inter-
> pret to us in all the Scriptures the things concern-
> ing himself.

It is not enough to possess a Bible, to read the Bible,
love the Bible, study the Bible, know the Bible. We
need to ask ourselves, Is the Christ of the Bible the cen-
ter of our lives? If not, all our Bible reading has been
futile, for this is the end to which the Bible is intended
to be the means.

3
The Holy Spirit & the Bible

ALL CHRISTIANS KNOW that the Holy Bible and the Holy Spirit are supposed to have something to do with one another. Indeed, all Christians believe that in some sense the Holy Bible is the creative product of the Holy Spirit. For whenever we say the Nicene Creed, we affirm as one of our beliefs about the Holy Spirit that "he spoke through the prophets." This expression echoes many similar phrases which occur in the New Testament. For example, our Lord Jesus once introduced a quotation from Psalm 110 with the words: "David himself, inspired by the Holy Spirit, declared . . ." (Mk 12:36). Similarly, the apostle Peter in his second letter wrote that "men moved by the Holy Spirit spoke from God" (2 Pet 1:21), or, as the Greek verb means, they were "carried along" by the Holy Spirit, as if by a powerful wind. There is then an important relationship between the Bible and the Spirit, one which we need to investigate.

So far we have considered that God is the author of the revelation that has been given and that Jesus Christ is its principal subject. Now we have to add that the Holy Spirit is its agent. Thus the Christian understanding of the Bible is essentially a Trinitarian understanding. The Bible comes from God, centers on Christ and is inspired by the Holy Spirit. So the best definition of the Bible is also Trinitarian: "The Bible is the witness of the Father to the Son through the Holy Spirit."

What then is the precise role of the Holy Spirit in the process of revelation? To answer this question we turn to the Bible itself and, in particular, to 1 Corinthians 2:6-16.

Yet among the mature we do impart wisdom, although it is not a wisdom of this age or of the rulers of this age, who are doomed to pass away. But we impart a secret and hidden wisdom of God, which God decreed before the ages for our glorification. None of the rulers of this age understood this; for if they had, they would not have crucified the Lord of glory. But, as it is written,

"What no eye has seen, nor ear heard,
nor the heart of man conceived,

what God has prepared for those who love him," God has revealed to us through the Spirit. For the Spirit searches everything, even the depths of God. For what person knows a man's thoughts except the spirit of the man which is in him? So also no one comprehends the thoughts of God except the Spirit of God. Now we have received not the spirit of the world, but the Spirit which is from God, that we might understand the gifts bestowed on us by God. And we impart this in words not taught by human wisdom but taught by the Spirit, interpreting spiritual truths to those who possess the Spirit.

The unspiritual man does not receive the gifts of the Spirit of God, for they are folly to him, and he is not able to understand them because they are spiritually discerned. The spiritual man judges all things, but is himself to be judged by no one. "For who has known the mind of the Lord so as to instruct him?" But we have the mind of Christ.

It is important that we see this text in its wider context. Up to this point in 1 Corinthians, Paul has been emphasizing the "foolishness" of the gospel. For example, "the word of the cross is *folly* to those who are perishing" (1:18), and "we preach Christ crucified, a stumbling block to Jews and *folly* to Gentiles" (1:23). Or, as we might put it today, the message of the cross sounds stupid to secular intellectuals, even meaningless. So Paul now adds a corrective, lest his readers should imagine that he is repudiating wisdom altogether and that he glories in folly instead. Is the apostle anti-intellectual, then? Does he scorn understanding and the use of the mind? No, indeed not.

Verses 6-7: "Yet among the mature we do impart wisdom, . . . a secret and hidden wisdom of God, which God decreed . . . for our glorification." The contrasts which Paul is making must not be overlooked. We *do* impart wisdom, he writes, but (1) only to the *mature*, not to non-Christians or even to very young Christians; (2) it is *God's* wisdom, not worldly wisdom; and (3) it is for our *glorification*, that is, our final perfection through sharing in God's glory, and not just to bring us to justification in Christ.

We ourselves need to follow the apostle's example. In evangelizing non-Christians we must concentrate on the foolishness of the gospel of Christ crucified for sinners. In building up Christians into full maturity, however, we should want to lead them into an understanding of God's total purpose. Paul calls this in verse 7 God's "secret and hidden wisdom" and in verse 9 "what God has prepared for those who love him." It can be known, he stresses, only by revelation. "The rulers of this age [secular leaders]" did not understand it, or they would never have crucified "the Lord of glory" (v. 8). They were not exceptional, however; all human beings, if left to themselves, are ignorant of God's wisdom and purpose.

For God's purpose, Paul writes in verse 9, is something which "no eye has seen" (it is invisible), "nor ear heard" (it is inaudible), "nor the heart of man conceived" (it is inconceivable). It is beyond the reach of human eyes, ears and minds. It is not amenable to scientific investigation, nor even to poetic imagination. It is altogether beyond our little finite minds to fathom unless God should reveal it. Which is exactly what God has done. Listen again: "What no eye has seen, nor ear heard, nor the heart of man conceived, what God has prepared for those who love him"—this unimaginable splendor of his purpose—"God has revealed to us through the Spirit." The word *us* is emphatic, and in the context it must refer not to all of us indiscriminately, but to the apostle Paul who is writing and to his fellow apostles. God gave a special revelation of these truths to special organs of revelation, the prophets in the Old Testament and the apostles in the New, and God did this "through the Spirit." The Holy Spirit has been the agent of this revelation.

All of this is, I'm afraid, a rather lengthy introduction to help us see the context within which Paul comes to his theme of the Holy Spirit as the agent of revelation. What he goes on to write is a marvelously comprehensive statement. He outlines the four stages of the Holy Spirit's work as agent of divine revelation.

The Searching Spirit
First, the Holy Spirit is the searching Spirit (vv. 10-11). It is worth noting, just in passing, that this shows the Holy Spirit to be personal. Only persons can engage in "search" or "research." To be sure, modern computers can undertake highly complex research of a mechanical, analytical kind. But true research, as all postgrad-

uate research students know well, involves more than
the compilation and analysis of statistical data; it re-
quires original thought, both in investigation and in
reflection. This then is work which the Holy Spirit
does, because he has a mind with which he thinks.
Since he is a divine Person (and not a computer, or a
vague influence or power), we need to accustom ourselves to referring to the Spirit as "he," not "it."

Paul uses two fascinating little pictures to indicate
the unique qualifications of the Holy Spirit in the work
of revelation. The first is that "the Spirit searches
everything, even the depths of God" (v. 10). It is the
same verb which Jesus applied to the Jews "searching
the scriptures," and Moulton and Milligan in their
Vocabulary of the Greek New Testament quote from a
third-century papyrus document in which the "search-
ers" appear to be customs officials. At any rate, the
Holy Spirit is depicted as a restlessly inquisitive research worker, or even (though *the depths* was a favorite
expression of Gnostic heretics, and Paul may be bor-
rowing it from their vocabulary) as a deep-sea diver
who is seeking to fathom the deepest depths of the
unfathomable Being of Almighty God. For God's
Being is infinite in its profundity, and Paul boldly
declares that the Spirit of God is searching the depths
of God. In other words, God himself is exploring the
riches of his own being.

The second model or picture Paul gives is taken
from human self-understanding. Verse 11 (NIV): "For
who among men knows the thoughts of a man except

the man's spirit within him?" *Thoughts* is literally
"things," a human being's "things," perhaps what we
would call our humanness. An ant cannot possibly con-
ceive what it is like to be a human being. Nor can a frog,
a rabbit or even the most intelligent ape. Nor can one
human being fully understand another human being.
How often we say, particularly in adolescence as we are
growing up, "You just don't understand; nobody understands me." That is true! Nobody does understand
me except myself, and even my understanding of myself is limited. In the same way nobody understands
you except yourself. This measure of self-understanding or self-consciousness Paul applies to the Holy
Spirit: "So also no one comprehends the thoughts of
God except the Spirit of God" (v. 11). The Holy Spirit
of God is here almost likened to the divine self-understanding or the divine self-consciousness. Just as
nobody can understand a human being except that
human being himself, so nobody can understand God
except God himself. We sometimes sing in a hymn,
"God only knows the love of God." We could equally
well affirm that only God knows the wisdom of God;
indeed only God knows the being of God.

So, then, the Spirit searches the depths of God, and
the Spirit knows the things of God. He has an understanding of God which is unique. The question now is
this: What has he done with what he has searched out
and come to know? Has he kept his unique knowledge
to himself? No. He has done what only he is competent
to do; he has revealed it. The searching spirit who

knows the depths of God became the revealing Spirit.

The Revealing Spirit

What the Holy Spirit alone has come to know, he alone
has made known. This has already been stated in verse
10: "God has revealed [it] to us [the apostles] through
the Spirit." Now Paul elaborates it in verse 12: "Now
we [it is the same apostolic "we," the plural of apostolic
authority] have received not the spirit of the world, but
the Spirit which is from God [namely, the searching
and knowing Spirit] that we might understand the
gifts bestowed on us by God." The apostles had, in
fact, received two gracious gifts from God, the first
his grace in salvation ("the gifts bestowed on us") and
the second his Spirit to enable them to understand his
gracious salvation.

Paul himself is the best example of this double
process. As we read his letters, he gives us a superb
exposition of the gospel of God's grace. He tells us
what God has done for guilty sinners like us who are
without excuse and deserve nothing from his hand but
judgment. He declares that God sent his Son to die for
our sins on the cross and to rise again, and that if we
are united to Jesus Christ, by faith inwardly and by
baptism outwardly, then we die with him and rise
again with him, and experience a new life in him. It is
a magnificent gospel that Paul unfolds in his letters.
But how does he know all this? How can he make such
comprehensive statements of salvation? The answer is,
first, that he has himself received it. He knows the

grace of God in experience. Then, second, the Holy Spirit has been given to him to interpret his own experience to him. Thus the Holy Spirit revealed to him God's plan of salvation, what Paul calls "the mystery" in other epistles. The searching Spirit became the revealing Spirit.

The Inspiring Spirit

Now we are ready for stage three: The revealing Spirit became the inspiring Spirit. Verse 13: "And we impart this in words not taught by human wisdom but taught by the Spirit." Notice that in verse 12 Paul writes of what "we have received," and in verse 13 of what "we impart." I might perhaps elaborate his sequence of thought like this: We have received these gracious gifts of God; we have received this Spirit to interpret to us what God has done for us and given to us; now we impart to others what we have received. The searching Spirit, who had revealed God's plan of salvation *to* the apostles, went on to communicate this gospel *through* the apostles to others.

Just as the Spirit did not keep his researches to himself, so the apostles did not keep his revelation to themselves. They understood that they were trustees of it. They had to deliver to others what they had received. Moreover, what they imparted or communicated was in words, and their words are specifically described as "not taught by human wisdom but taught by the Spirit" (v. 13). See how the Holy Spirit is mentioned again, this time as the inspiring Spirit. Here in verse 13 is an un-

ambiguous claim on the part of the apostle Paul to
verbal inspiration. That is to say, the very words with
which the apostles clothed the message that had been
revealed to them by the Spirit were words taught them
by the same Spirit.

I strongly suspect that the reason the notion of verbal inspiration is unpopular today is that people misunderstand it. What they are rejecting, in consequence, is not its true meaning but a caricature. So let
me try to clear the concept of some major misconcep-
tions. First, verbal inspiration does not mean that
every word of the Bible is literally true. We fully recog-
nize that the biblical authors used many different literary genres, each of which must be interpreted according to its own rules—history as history, poetry as poetry, parable as parable, and so on. What is inspired is
the *natural* sense of the words according to the author's
intention, whether it be literal or figurative.

Second, verbal inspiration does not mean verbal
dictation. Muslims believe that Allah dictated the
Qur'an to Mohammed, word by word, in Arabic.
Christians do not believe this about the Bible, for, as we
have already seen and as I shall further emphasize
later, the Holy Spirit treated the biblical authors as
persons, not machines. With a few minor exceptions
they seem to have been in full possession of their faculties while the Spirit was communicating his Word
through their words.

Third, verbal inspiration does not mean that every
sentence of the Bible, in isolation from its context, is

God's Word. For not everything contained in the Bible is affirmed by the Bible. We see a good example in the long speeches of Job's so-called comforters. Their major thesis, repeated ad nauseam, namely, that God was punishing Job for his personal sins, was mistaken. In the last chapter God says to them twice, "You have not spoken of me what is right" (42:7-8). So their words cannot be taken as God's words. They are included in order to be contradicted, not endorsed. The inspired Word of God is what is being affirmed, whether as instruction, command or promise.

Verbal inspiration means that what the Holy Spirit has spoken and still speaks through the human authors, understood according to the plain, natural meaning of the words used, is true and without error. There is no need at all to be embarrassed by this Christian belief, or to be ashamed or afraid of it. On the contrary, it is eminently reasonable, because words are the units of which sentences are made up. Words are the building blocks of speech. It is therefore impossible to frame a precise message without constructing precise sentences composed of precise words.

Think of the trouble we all take to compose a cable or telegram. Let us say we've got only twelve words. All the same, we are determined to send a message which will not only be understood, but which will not be misunderstood. So we draft it, redraft it and draft it again. We scratch out a word here and we add a word there until we have polished our message to our satisfaction. Words matter. Every speaker who wants to

communicate a message that will be understood and
not misunderstood knows the importance of words.
Every preacher who takes pains to prepare his sermons chooses his words with care. Every writer,
whether of letters or articles or books, knows that
words matter. Listen to what Charles Kingsley said in
the middle of the last century: "These glorious things
—words—are man's right alone. . . . Without words
we should know no more of each other's hearts and
thoughts than the dog knows of his fellow dog . . . for,
if you will consider, you always think to yourself in
words, though you do not speak them aloud; and without them all our thoughts would be mere blind long-
ings, feelings which we could not understand ourselves." We have to clothe them in words.

This then is the apostolic claim: that the same Holy
Spirit of God, who searches the depths of God and revealed his researches to the apostles, went on to communicate them through the apostles in words with
which he himself supplied them. He spoke his words
through their words so that they were equally the
words of God and the words of man. This is the double
authorship of Scripture, which I have already mentioned. It is also the meaning of "inspiration." The
inspiration of Scripture was not a mechanical process
that bypassed God's personhood or the writers'. It was
intensely personal; for it involved a Person, the Holy
Spirit, speaking through persons, prophets and apostles, in such a way that his words were theirs and their
words were his simultaneously.

The Enlightening Spirit

We come now to the fourth stage in the Holy Spirit's work as the agent of revelation, and in this I shall describe him as the "enlightening" Spirit. Let me set the scene.

How are we to think about the people who heard the apostles preaching and later read their letters? Were they left to fend for themselves? Were they obliged to struggle as best they could to understand the apostolic message? No. The same Spirit who was active in those who wrote the apostolic letters was also active in those who read them. Thus the Holy Spirit was working at both ends, as it were, inspiring the apostles and enlightening their hearers. This is already implied at the end of 1 Corinthians 2:13, a complicated phrase which has been variously interpreted. I take the Revised Standard Version translation as correct, namely, that the Holy Spirit was "interpreting spiritual truths to those who possess the Spirit." Possession of the Spirit was not limited to the biblical authors. Certainly his work of inspiration in them was unique; yet to it he added his work of interpretation.

Verses 14 and 15 elaborate this truth, and they are in stark contrast to each other. Verse 14 begins by referring to "the unspiritual man" (or "the natural man," KJV), that is, the unregenerate person who is not a Christian. Verse 15, however, begins with a reference to "the spiritual man," the possessor of the Holy Spirit. Paul thus divides humanity into two clear-cut categories: the natural and the spiritual, that is, those who

possess natural, animal or physical life, on the one
hand, and on the other those who have received
spiritual or eternal life. The first category lack the
Holy Spirit because they have never been born again,
but the Holy Spirit dwells in those to whom he has
given a new birth. The indwelling of the Holy Spirit is,
in fact, the distinguishing mark of the true Christian
man and woman (Rom 8:9).

What difference does it make whether we have the
Holy Spirit or not? All the difference in the world—
especially, although there are other distinctions, to our
understanding of spiritual truth. The unspiritual or
unregenerate person, who has not received the Holy
Spirit, does not receive the things of the Spirit either,
because they are foolishness to him or her (1 Cor 2:14).
Not only does he fail to understand them; he is not even
able to do so because they are "spiritually discerned."
Spiritual persons, on the other hand, born-again
Christians in whom the Holy Spirit dwells, "discern"
(it is the same Greek verb as in verse 14) "all things."
Not, of course, that they become omniscient like God,
but that all those things to which they were previously
blind, and which God has revealed in Holy Scripture,
begin to make sense to them. They understand what
they have never understood before, even though they
themselves are not really understood. Literally, they
are "discerned by no one." They remain an enigma,
for they have an inner secret of spiritual life and truth
which doesn't make sense to nonbelievers. This is
hardly surprising, however, for nobody knows the

mind of the Lord or can instruct him. And since non-believers cannot understand Christ's mind, they cannot understand ours either, though we whom the Holy Spirit enlightens can dare to say, "We have the mind of Christ" (v. 16)—a truly amazing affirmation.

Is this your experience? Has the Bible become a new book to you? William Grimshaw, one of the great eighteenth-century evangelical leaders, told a friend after his conversion that "if God had drawn up his Bible to heaven, and sent him down another, it could not have been newer to him." It was a different book. I could say the same myself. I read the Bible daily before I was converted, because my mother brought me up to do so, but it was double Dutch to me. I hadn't the foggiest idea what it was all about. But when I was born again and the Holy Spirit came to dwell within me, the Bible immediately *began* to be a new book to me. Of course I am not claiming that I understood everything. I am far from understanding everything today. But I began to understand things I had never understood before.

What a marvelous experience this is! Don't think of the Bible as just a collection of musty old documents whose real place is in a library. Don't think of the pages of Scripture as if they were fossils whose real place is behind glass in a museum. No, God speaks through what he has spoken. Through the ancient text of Scripture the Holy Spirit can communicate with us today freshly, personally and powerfully. "He who has an ear, let him hear what the Spirit says" ("is saying"—it

is a present tense—through the Scriptures) "to the
churches" (Rev 2:7 and so on).

If the Holy Spirit speaks to us through the Scriptures today, you may be asking, why don't we all agree
about everything? If the Spirit is the interpreter as well
as the agent of God's revelation, why does he not lead
us to a common mind? My answer to these questions
may surprise you. It is that he does in fact enable us to
agree much more than we disagree, and that we would
agree with one another even more if we fulfilled the
following four conditions.

First, we must accept the supreme authority of
Scripture and earnestly desire to submit to it. Among
those who do so, a substantial Christian consensus already exists. The big and painful differences which
remain, for example, between the Roman Catholic
Church and the Protestant churches are mainly attrib-
utable to the former's continuing unwillingness to
declare that Scripture has supreme authority even
over church traditions. Rome's official position, modi-
fied but not effectively altered by the Second Vatican
Council, is still that "both Sacred Tradition and Sacred
Scripture are to be accepted and venerated with the
same sense of devotion and reverence." Now Protestants do not deny the importance of tradition, and
some of us should have more respect for it since the
Holy Spirit has taught past generations of Christians
and did not begin his instruction only with us! Nevertheless, when Scripture and tradition are in collision,
we must allow Scripture to reform tradition, just as

Jesus insisted with the "traditions of the elders" (see Mk 7:1-13). If the Church of Rome were to have the courage to renounce unbiblical traditions, such as its dogmas about the immaculate conception and bodily assumption of the Virgin Mary, immediate progress would be made toward agreement under the Word of God.

Second, we must remember that, as we have seen, the overriding purpose of Scripture is to bear witness to Christ as the all-sufficient Savior of sinners. When the sixteenth-century Reformers insisted on the "perspicuity" (that is, clarity) of Scripture, and translated the Bible into the vernacular so that ordinary people could read it for themselves, they were referring to the way of salvation. They did not deny that the Scriptures contain "some things . . . hard to understand," as Peter said of Paul's letters (2 Pet 3:16); what they were at pains to affirm was that the essential truths of salvation were plain for all to understand.

Third, we must apply sound principles of interpretation. It is of course perfectly possible to twist the Bible into meaning anything we like. But our business is Scripture interpreting, not Scripture twisting. Above all, we have to seek both the *original* sense according to the biblical author's intention, and the *natural* sense, which may be either literal or figurative, again according to the author's intention. These are respectively the principles of history and of simplicity. When they are applied with integrity and rigor, then the Bible controls us and not we it. In consequence, the area of Christian agreement increases.

Fourth, we must come to the biblical text with a recognition of our cultural prejudices and with a willingness to have them challenged and changed. If we come to Scripture with the proud presupposition that all our inherited beliefs and practices are correct, then of course we shall find in the Bible only what we want to find, namely, the comfortable confirmation of the status quo. As a result we shall also find ourselves in sharp disagreement with people who come to Scripture from different backgrounds and with different convictions, and find their beliefs confirmed. There is probably no commoner source of discord than this. It is only when we are brave and humble enough to allow the Spirit of God through the Word of God radically to call into question our most cherished opinions that we are likely to find fresh unity through fresh understanding.

The "spiritual discernment" which the Holy Spirit promises is not given in defiance of these four common-sense conditions; it presupposes that they are accepted and fulfilled.

Conclusion

We have considered the Holy Spirit in four roles, as the searching Spirit, the revealing Spirit, the inspiring Spirit and the enlightening Spirit. These are the four stages of his teaching ministry. First, he searches the depths of God and knows the thoughts of God. Second, he revealed his researches to the apostles. Third, he communicated *through* the apostles what he had revealed *to* them, and did so in words that he himself supplied. Fourth, he enlightened the minds of the hearers so that they could discern what he had revealed to and through the apostles, and he continues this work of illumination today in those who are willing to receive it.

Let me give two very simple and short lessons. The first concerns our view of the Holy Spirit. There is much discussion today about the person and work of the Spirit, and 1 Corinthians 2:6-16 is only one of many passages in the Bible about him. But let me ask you this: Is there room in your doctrine of the Spirit for this passage? Jesus called him "the Spirit of truth." So truth is very important to the Holy Spirit. Oh, I know, he is also the Spirit of holiness, the Spirit of love and the Spirit of power, but is he to you the Spirit of *truth*? According to the verses we have been studying, he is deeply concerned about the truth. He searches it, has revealed and communicated it, and enlightens our minds to grasp it. Dear friend, never denigrate truth! Never disdain theology! Never despise your mind! If you do, you grieve the Holy Spirit of truth. This passage should affect our view of the Holy Spirit.

The second concerns our need of the Holy Spirit. Do you want to grow in your knowledge of God? Of course you do. Do you want to grow in your understanding of the wisdom of God and of the totality of his purpose to make us one day like Christ in glory? Of course you do. So do I. Then we need the Holy Spirit, the Spirit of truth, to illumine our minds. For that we need to be born again. I sometimes wonder if the reason some secular theologians today are speaking and writing, if I may say so, such rubbish (I am referring, for example, to their denial of personality to God and of deity to Jesus) is that they have never been born again. It is possible to be a theologian and unregenerate. Is that why they do not discern these marvelous truths of Scripture? Scripture is spiritually discerned. So we need to come to the Scriptures humbly, reverently and expectantly. We need to acknowledge that the truths revealed in the Bible are still locked and sealed until the Holy Spirit opens them to us and opens our minds to them. For God hides them from the wise and clever and reveals them only to "babes," those who are humble and reverent in their approach to him. So then, before we preachers prepare, before a congregation listens, before an individual or a group begins to read the Bible—in these situations we must pray for the Holy Spirit's illumination: "Open my eyes that I may see wonderful things in your law" (Ps 119: 18 NIV). And he will.

4
The Church
& the
Bible

S O FAR WE HAVE ENGAGED in a Trinitarian study.
We have seen that God is the author, Christ both the
principal subject and the authenticating witness, and
the Holy Spirit the agent of the great process of revelation. We come now to the church.

What do you think of the church? Your answer will
probably depend on whether you are thinking about
the ideal or the reality. In the ideal the church is the
most marvelous new creation of God. It is the new
community of Jesus, enjoying a multiracial, multi-
national and multicultural harmony which is unique
in history and in contemporary society. The church is

even the "new humanity," the vanguard of a redeemed and renewed human race. It is a people who
spend their earthly lives, as they will also spend eternity, in the loving service of God and of others. What a
noble and beautiful ideal! In reality, however, the
church is us (if you will pardon the bad grammar)—
a disheveled rabble of sinful, fallible, bickering, squabbling, stupid, shallow Christians, who constantly fall
short of God's ideal and often fail even to approximate
to it.

What is the reason for this gulf between the ideal
and the reality? Why is the church in such a perilous
condition throughout the world today—weak, frag-
mented and making so little impact on the world for
Christ? I'm sure there are many reasons, but I believe
the overwhelming reason is what Amos called "a
famine . . . of hearing the words of the LORD" (Amos
8:11), or in plain modern language, a neglect of the
Bible. The multiple unfaithfulness of the church is
due to its overriding unfaithfulness to the self-revelation of God in Scripture. The late Dr. Martyn Lloyd-
Jones was right when he wrote in his book *Preaching
and Preachers* (1971) that "the decadent eras and
periods of the Church's history have always been those
in which preaching has declined." In other words, the
church remains sick and feeble whenever it refuses the
healing medicine and wholesome nourishment of the
Word of God.

We are now going to consider two texts, both of
which use an architectural metaphor. In Ephesians

2:20 the church, which has just been defined as God's "household" or family (v. 19), is further described as "built upon the foundation of the apostles and prophets, Christ Jesus himself being the cornerstone." That is, the teaching of the biblical authors is the foundation on which the church is built, as Jesus Christ is the cornerstone which holds it together. In 1 Timothy 3:15 the metaphor is reversed. Having again referred to the church as "the household of God," Paul now goes on to call it "the pillar and foundation of the truth" (NIV).

You will observe that in the first text the truth is the foundation, and the church is the building it supports, while in the second text the church is the foundation and the truth is the building which it supports.

"Well, there you are," I hear somebody saying, "I told you so. The Bible is full of contradictions." Really? Wait a moment. Both these verses come from the pen of the same man, the apostle Paul. Let us give him credit for a little logical consistency. It has always been dangerous to use metaphors and similes. We have to inquire at what point the analogy is being made in order to understand what the author is intending to say through the figure of speech that he is using. When we apply this principle to our two texts, we find, as we would expect, that they are beautifully complementary.

You ask how at one and the same time the truth can be the foundation of the church and the church the foundation of the truth? Well, let me suggest the answer. What Paul is affirming in Ephesians 2:20 is that the church depends upon the truth for its existence. It rests upon the teaching of the apostles and prophets, and without their teaching, now recorded in Scripture, the church could neither exist nor survive, let alone flourish. But according to 1 Timothy 3:15 the truth depends on the church for its defense and propagation. The church is called to serve the truth by holding it firm against attack and by holding it high before the eyes of the world. Thus the church *needs* the Bible because it is built on it. And the church *serves* the Bible by holding it fast and making it known. These are the two complementary truths that we are going to investigate further.

The Church Needs the Bible
The church's dependence on the Bible is manifold. Let me give you a number of examples.

1. The Bible created the church.   Put thus baldly, this statement could be misleading. It could even be dismissed as inaccurate. For it is true that the Old Testament church as the people of God existed for centuries before the Bible was complete. Furthermore, the New Testament church also existed for a long time before the New Testament canon was finalized, and longer still before the first Bible was printed for publications. Moreover, you may rightly say, the first-century church "shaped" the New Testament in the sense that the Christian community shared in determining in what form the words and works of Jesus would be preserved for posterity. The church was thus the milieu within which the Bible came to be written and treasured. I agree with all these qualifications. Nevertheless, I repeat, the Bible may be said to have created the church. Or, more accurately, the Word of God, which is now written in the Bible, created the church. For how did the Christian church come into being? Answer: By the preaching of the apostles, who spoke not in the name of the church, but in the name of Christ.

On the Day of Pentecost Peter added his apostolic testimony to the prophetic witness of the Old Testament, he proclaimed Jesus as Messiah and Lord, the Holy Spirit confirmed his words with power, and the believing people of God became the Spirit-filled body of Christ. God himself performed this creative work by his Spirit through his Word. Moreover he continued to honor the preaching of the apostles in the same way. On his famous missionary journeys Paul also bore witness to Christ, arguing that the testimony of the apostolic eyewitnesses was in full harmony with the Old Testament Scriptures. Many listened, repented, believed and were baptized, so that churches were planted all over the Roman Empire. How? By the Word of God.

God's Word (the combined witness of prophets and apostles), proclaimed in the power of the Spirit, created the church. It still does. The church is built on that foundation. And when the canon of the New Testament came to be determined, the church did not confer authority on these documents, but simply acknowledged the authority they already possessed.

Why? Because they were "apostolic" and contained the teaching of the Lord's apostles. For these reasons, we may truthfully say that the Bible, that is, the Word of God now written in the Bible, created and creates the church.

2. The Bible sustains the church. The Creator always sustains what he has created, and since he has brought the church into being, he keeps it in being. Moreover, having created it by his Word, he sustains and nourishes it by his Word. If it is true, as Jesus said quoting Deuteronomy (Mt 4:4; compare Deut 8:3), that human beings live "not by bread alone, but by every word that proceeds from the mouth of God," it is also true of churches. They cannot flourish without it. The church needs constantly to hear God's Word. Hence the central place of preaching in public worship. Preaching is not an intrusion into it, but rather indispensable to it. For the worship of God is always a response to the Word of God. That is why, for example, in all the worship services of the Church of England, there is an oscillation between Word and worship. First God speaks his Word in Scripture sentence, readings and exposition, and then the people respond in confession, creed, praise and prayer. The Christian congregation grows into maturity in Jesus Christ only as they hear, receive, believe, absorb and obey the Word of God.

3. The Bible directs the church. The Christian community is a pilgrim people on its way to an eternal home. It is traveling through territory that is barren, pathless, hostile and dark. It needs guidance for the way, and God has provided it. "Your word is a lamp to my feet and a light for my path" (Ps 119:105 NIV). I agree, of course, that what is called the hermeneutical task, that is, the task of interpreting the Scriptures, is difficult. Scripture does not give us slick answers to complex twentieth-century problems. We have to wrestle with the text, with both its meaning and its application, and do so in prayer, study and fellowship with each other. Nevertheless, the principles we need to guide us are there in the Bible—theological and ethical principles—and together we can discover through the illumination of the Holy Spirit how to apply them to our lives in the contemporary world.

4. The Bible reforms the church.   In every century, including our own, I am sorry to say, the church has deviated to some degree from God's truth and from his ethical standards. As Max Warren, the former missionary statesman, wrote in his book *I Believe in the Great Commission*, church history is "a bitter-sweet story" in which the most outstanding fact is the infinite patience of God with his people. If then the church is constantly deviant, how can it be reformed? Only by the Word of God. The greatest church renewal there has ever been in the history of the world was the sixteenth-century Reformation, and it was due, more than anything else, to a recovery of the Bible.

5. The Bible unites the church.   Every Christian conscience should be troubled by the disunity of the church. I hope we have not grown accustomed to it or

begun to acquiesce in it. The visible unity of the
church, although we may not all agree with one another what precise form it should take, is surely a
proper goal of Christian endeavor.

What then is the basic reason for our continuing
disunity? It is the lack of an agreed authority. So long
as churches follow their own traditions and specula-
tions, the universal church will continue to splinter.
For example, the Anglican Church, to which I belong,
is at fault in this matter. In its negotiations for unity or
reunion, it insists on what it calls the "historic episcopate" as a non-negotiable item, and not only so, but
often on a particular "catholic" interpretation of the
episcopate known as the "apostolic succession." Now
all of us believe in *episkopē,* the New Testament word
for the pastoral oversight of the church. And a good
historical, pastoral and practical case can be made out
for an episcopal form of government as being conducive to the well-being of the church. But it certainly
cannot be made indispensable, for the simple reason
that it is not required in Scripture. It can be defended
as being consistent with biblical teaching and pastoral
care. But that is another matter. In so far as the
Church of England insists on the historic episcopate
as non-negotiable, it is hindering the unity of the
church. Once churches confess the supreme authority
of Scripture, however, and its sole sufficiency for
salvation, and are determined to judge their traditions
by its teaching, then at once the way is opened for them
to find unity in truth. The Bible unites the church

when the church submits to it.

6. *The Bible revives the church.* We long for revival, for that special, unusual, supernatural visitation by God, as a result of which the whole community becomes aware of his living and holy presence. Sinners are convicted, penitents converted, backsliders restored, enemies reconciled, believers transformed, and dead churches revivified. But how does revival happen? Only, it is true, by a sovereign work of the Holy Spirit of God. But what means does the Holy Spirit use? He uses his Word. The Word of God is "the sword of the Spirit" which he wields in his work in the world (Eph 6:17; compare Heb 4:12). Never separate the Spirit of God from the Word of God, for when the Holy Spirit uses this weapon in his sovereign power, he pricks the conscience, cuts out cancerous growths from the body of Christ and puts the devil to flight. It is the Bible that revives the church.

Are you convinced? I hope so. The church needs the Bible. The church depends on the Bible. The church is built upon the foundation of the apostles and prophets. The Bible is indispensable to the church's life, growth, nature, direction, reformation, unity and renewal. The church cannot exist without the Bible.

This leads to the second and complementary truth: If the church needs the Bible, the Bible also needs the church. If the church depends on the Bible, the Bible also depends on the church. For the church is called to serve the Bible by guarding and spreading its message.

The Church Serves the Bible

Although God spoke his Word through prophets and
apostles, it had to be received and written down. Today it still needs to be translated, printed, published,
distributed, preached, defended, broadcast, televised
and dramatized. In these and other ways the church is
serving the Bible, guarding it and making it known.

This explains why Paul wrote in 1 Timothy 3:15 that
the church is "the pillar and ground of the truth."
The two Greek words he used are instructive. The first
is *stylos*, which undoubtedly means a pillar or column.
The meaning of the other word *(hedraiōma)* is not so
certain, and has been variously translated into English
as "ground" (KJV), "bulwark" (RSV), "buttress" (NEB)
and "foundation" (NIV). It comes from the adjective
hedraios which means "firm, steady, stable," even "immovable" (it was used of mountains). So the noun
hedraiōma could be used of any kind of support or sta-
bilizer. When applied to a building, therefore, it could
refer either to its foundation or to a buttress, since
the purpose of both is to keep the building stable.

Now let us put these two ideas together. The church
is both the foundation or buttress of the truth on the
one hand, and the pillar of the truth on the other.
Foundations and buttresses hold a building firm;
pillars hold it high, thrusting it aloft for people to see.
This suggests respectively the apologetic task and the
evangelistic task of the church. For, as the foundation
or buttress of the truth, the church must hold it firm
and defend it against heretics so that the truth remains

steadfast and immovable. But, as the pillar of the truth, the church must hold it high, making it visible to the world so that people may see it and believe. So the Bible needs the church to protect it and to propagate it.

I am glad that the twentieth article of the Anglican Thirty-Nine Articles describes the church as "a witness and a keeper of Holy Writ." There is an urgent need for both these responsibilities. On the one hand, heresy is gaining ground in the church. There are false teachers who deny the infinite, loving personality of Almighty God and others who deny the deity of our Lord Jesus Christ, as well as the authority of the Bible. These heretics seem to be increasing, and are spreading their pernicious ideas by books and sermons, on radio and television. So the truth needs buttresses— Christian scholars who will give their lives to what Paul called "the defense and confirmation of the gospel" (Phil 1:7). Is God calling some younger theologian who is reading these words to be a buttress of the truth in the church, to hold it firm, to defend it against heresy and misunderstanding? What a vocation! The church must guard and demonstrate the truth.

At the same time the church is called to preach the gospel throughout the world. There are some three thousand million people in the world who have never really heard of Jesus, and there are many more who, having heard of him, have never believed in him. "How are they to hear without a preacher?" (Rom 10: 14). The church needs pioneer evangelists who will develop new forms of mission in order to penetrate closed areas, especially the Islamic, the Marxist and the secular worlds. For the church is the pillar of the truth. We've got to hold it high and make it known so that people may see it in its beauty and adequacy, and embrace it for themselves.

Conclusion

The church needs the Bible and the Bible needs the church. Those are the complementary truths which Paul's two statements express. The church could not survive without the Bible to sustain it, and the Bible could hardly survive without the church to guard and spread it. Each needs the other. The Bible and the church are twins, inseparable Siamese twins. Once we have got hold of that, we are ready for a threefold exhortation.

First, I exhort Christian pastors (including myself) to take our preaching more seriously. Our calling is to study and expound the Word of God and relate it to the modern world. The health of every congregation depends more than anything else on the quality of its preaching ministry. This may surprise you. I know, of course, that church members can grow into maturity in Christ in spite of their pastors, and even when their pastors are bad or neglectful. For they can pray and read the Scriptures both by themselves and in fellowship groups, and nowadays good books and cassettes are available as a valuable supplementary means of instruction. Nevertheless, the New Testament indicates that God's purpose is to commit the care of his people to pastors, who are so to proclaim Christ to them out of the Scriptures, in the glory of his person and work, that their worship, faith and obedience are drawn out from them. That is why I dare to say that, more often than not, the pew is a reflection of the pulpit, and that the pew does not normally rise higher than the pulpit. So then, my fellow pastors, let us determine afresh to give ourselves to this priority task!

Second, I exhort Christian people not only to study the Bible themselves in their homes and in their fellowship groups, but to demand (it is not too strong a word) faithful, biblical preaching from their pastors. Let me put it like this: the ministry you get is the ministry you deserve, and the ministry you deserve is the ministry you demand. Lay people have much more power in the churches than they commonly realize. They join a church where the Bible is hardly ever preached, and give in to it, acquiesce in it, do nothing about it! There may be times when you need to have the courage to reprove your pastors because you perceive that they are not being diligent in their study and faithful in their exposition. But don't give us only your reproof; give us your encouragement and your prayers. Set your pastors free from the distracting burden of administration. Pastoral oversight should also be shared by the lay leaders of the congregation. Every generation needs to relearn the lesson of Acts 6, where the apostles refused to be deflected from the teaching role to which Christ had called them. They delegated certain social and administrative tasks in order to devote themselves "to prayer and to the ministry of the word" (Acts 6:1-6). It is the lay leaders of the congregation who can ensure that the same priority is recognized today.

Third, I want to exhort Christian parents. Teach the Bible to your children. Don't surrender this parental responsibility to the school or even to the church; do it yourself, so that your children, like Timothy, come to know the Holy Scriptures from childhood (2 Tim 3:15). If you do this, then the next generation of church leaders that arise will grasp, as the present generation does not seem to, the indispensable place of the Bible in the church.

So let us enthrone the Bible in the home and in the church, not because we worship it but because God speaks through it. Then, as we hear his voice again, the church will be renewed, reformed and revived, and it will become what God has always intended it to be—a bright light shining in the prevailing darkness.

5
The Christian & the Bible

LET ME REHEARSE BRIEFLY the territory which we have traversed. We have thought about God and the Bible because he is its author, about Christ and the Bible because he is its subject, about the Holy Spirit and the Bible because he was the means of its inspiration, and about the church and the Bible because the church is built upon it and is called to guard its treasures and make them known. We conclude with something more personal and individual: the Christian and the Bible.

I do not hesitate to say that the Bible is indispensable to every Christian's health and growth. Christians who neglect the Bible simply do not mature. When Jesus quoted from Deuteronomy to the effect that human beings do not live by bread only but by God's Word, he was asserting that the Word of God is just as necessary for spiritual health as food is for bodily health. I am not now thinking of remote Christian tribespeople into whose language the Bible has not yet been translated, nor of illiterate people who may have the Bible in their language but are unable to read it for themselves. To be sure, such people are not altogether cut off from the nourishment of God's Word, for they can still receive it, though at one or two removes, from a missionary, pastor, relative or friend. I am bound to say, however, that I think their Christian life would be enriched if they could have direct access to the Scriptures, which is why such heroic work has been done to have the Bible translated into the languages of the world. I am not thinking of these situations. I am thinking rather about ourselves. We have a plethora of Bibles in a variety of editions and versions. Our problem is not that the Bible is unavailable to us, but that we do not take advantage of its availability. We need to read and meditate on it daily, to study it in a fellowship group and to hear it expounded during Sunday worship. Otherwise we shall not grow. Growth into maturity in Christ depends upon a close acquaintance with, and a believing response to, the Bible.

I want to try to answer the question which may be forming in your minds: just how and why does the

Bible enable us to grow? As an illustration of its effectiveness as a means of grace, I have chosen the story of Jesus' washing of his apostles' feet, recorded in John 13. When he had finished, put on his outer garment again and returned to his place, he immediately referred to himself as their teacher. "You call me Teacher and Lord; and you are right, for so I am" (v. 13). The implication is clear, that through his act of foot washing he had been teaching them certain truths and lessons which he wanted them to learn. There seem to have been three.

1. He was teaching them about himself. Jesus' actions were a deliberate parable of his mission. John seems clearly to have understood this for he introduces the incident with these words. "Jesus, knowing . . . that he had come from God and was going to God, rose from supper . . ." (vv. 3-4). That is, knowing these things, he dramatized them in action. Perhaps the best commentary is Philippians 2, which unfolds the stages of his self-humbling before he was highly exalted. Thus Jesus "rose from supper," as he had risen from his heavenly throne. He "laid aside his garments," as he had laid aside his glory and emptied himself of it. He then "girded himself with a towel" (the badge of servitude), as in the Incarnation he had taken the form of a servant. Next, he began "to wash the disciples' feet, and to wipe them with the towel," as he went to the cross to secure our cleansing from sin. After this he put his garments back on "and resumed his place," as he returned to his heavenly glory and sat down at the Father's right hand. By these actions he was dramatizing his whole earthly career. He was teaching them about himself, who he was, where he had come from and where he was going.

2. *He was teaching them about his salvation.* He said to Peter, "Unless I wash you, you have no part with me" (13:8 NIV). In other words, the forgiveness of sin is a necessary prelude to fellowship with Jesus Christ. Unless and until we have been washed, we cannot have anything to do with him. More subtly still, Jesus distinguished between two different kinds of washing: the bath on the one hand, and the washing of feet on the other. The apostles were familiar with this social distinction. Before visiting a friend's home, they would take a bath. Then on arrival at their friend's, a servant would wash their feet. They would not need another bath, but only a foot washing. Jesus seems to have used this well-known cultural distinction to teach a less well-known theological distinction: when we first come to him in penitence and faith we get a bath and are washed all over. Theologically, it is called "justification" or "regeneration," and is symbolized in baptism. Then, when we fall into sin as Christians, what we need is not another bath (we cannot be rejustified or rebaptized) but a foot washing, that is, the cleansing of a daily forgiveness. So Jesus says in verse 10 (NIV), "A person who has had a bath needs only to wash his feet; his whole body is clean."

3. *He was teaching them about his will.* We know from the synoptic Gospels that, before sitting down for the meal in the upper room, the apostles had been squabbling about who was to have the best seats. They were so preoccupied with questions of precedence that they sat down to the meal unwashed. Evidently there had been no servant to wash their feet, and it had not occurred to them that one of them might assume that lowly role and wash the feet of the others. So during supper Jesus did what none of them would have demeaned himself to do. And when he had finished, he said to them, "If I then, your Lord and Teacher, have washed your feet, you also ought to wash one another's feet. For I have given you an example, that you also should do as I have done to you. Truly, truly, I say to you, a servant is not greater than his master. . . . If you know these things, blessed are you if you do them" (vv. 14–17). Our Lord stooped to serve. It is his will that we do so too.

Here, then, were Jesus' three lessons from one incident: first about his person, that he had come from God and was going to God; second about his salvation, that after the bath of justification we need only the continuous washing of our feet; and third about his will, that we must wash one another's feet, that is, express our love for one another in humble service. Or, put another way, he taught three lessons which required three responses. In giving them a revelation of himself, he was asking for their worship. In giving them a promise of salvation, he was asking for their trust. In giving them a commandment to love and serve one another, he was asking for their obedience.

I do not think it an exaggeration to claim that all the teaching of the Bible can be divided into these three categories, requiring these three responses. Throughout Scripture there are revelations of God demanding our worship, promises of salvation demanding our faith and commandments about our duty demanding our obedience. Having considered the foot washing as one example, let us look at this threefold pattern a little more fully.

Revelations of God

The Bible is God's self-disclosure, the divine autobiography. In the Bible the subject and the object are identical, for in it God is speaking about God. He makes himself known progressively in the rich variety of his being: as the Creator of the universe and of human beings in his own image, the climax of his creation; as the living God who sustains and animates everything he has made; as the covenant God who chose Abraham, Isaac, Jacob and their descendants to be his special people; and as a gracious God who is slow to anger and quick to forgive, but also as a righteous God who punishes idolatry and injustice among his own people as well as in the pagan nations. Then in the New Testament he reveals himself as the Father of our Lord and Savior Jesus Christ, the One who sent him into the world to take our nature upon him, to be born and grow, live and teach, work and suffer, die and rise, occupy the throne and send the Holy Spirit. Next he shows himself as the God of the new covenant community, the church, who sends his people into the world as his witnesses and his servants in the power of the Holy Spirit. Finally he reveals himself as the God who one day will send Jesus Christ in power and glory to save, to judge and to reign, who will create a new universe and who in the end will be everything to everybody.

This majestic revelation of God—Father, Son and Holy Spirit—which unfolds from the creation to the consummation, moves us to worship. When we catch these glimpses of the greatness of God, of his glory and grace, we fall down on our faces before him and bring to him the homage of our lips, our hearts and our lives. It is impossible to read the Bible with any sensitivity and not be a worshiper. The Word of God evokes the worship of God.

Promises of Salvation

We have already seen that God's main purpose in giving us the Bible is to "instruct [us] for salvation through faith in Christ Jesus" (2 Tim 3:15). So the Bible tells the story of Jesus, foretelling and foreshadowing him in the Old Testament, describing his earthly career in the Gospels, and unfolding in the Epistles the fullness of his person and work. But it does more. The Scripture does not just present Jesus to us as our all-sufficient Savior; it urges us to go to him and put our trust in him. And it promises us that, if we do so, we shall receive the forgiveness of our sins and the gift of the liberating Holy Spirit. The Bible is full of salvation promises. It pledges new life in the new community to those who respond to the call of Jesus Christ. Jesus gave one such promise to Peter in the incident of the foot washing when he said to him, "You are clean" (Jn 13:10). Peter's mind must often have grasped that promise and believed it. Even after he had denied Jesus, he was not repudiated. Of course, he needed to repent, to be forgiven, to be recommissioned. But he did not need another bath, since already he had been made clean. The words of Jesus must have reassured his heart and pacified his nagging conscience.

Do you remember how in *Pilgrim's Progress,* after the disastrous experience in Bypath Meadow, Christian and Hopeful found themselves on the grounds of Doubting Castle? Its owner was Giant Despair, who found them asleep when they should have been praying. He then "put them into his castle," writes Bunyan, "in a very dark dungeon, nasty and stinking to the spirits of these two men. Here, then, they lay from Wednesday morning till Saturday night, without one bit of bread, or drop of drink, or light, or any to ask them how they did." In the morning, at his wife's instigation, Giant took "a grievous crab-tree cudgel," and "fell upon them and beat them fearfully"—with doubts, of course. The next day his wife advised him "to counsel them to make away with themselves," which Giant did, "either with knife, halter or poison." That is, since they were never likely to escape, they might as well take their own lives. Giant Despair is always whispering to his victims about suicide. On the third day he took them into the castle yard and showed them the bones and skulls of their predecessors. "These," he said with glee, "were pilgrims, as you are, once, and they trespassed on my grounds, as you have done; and when I saw fit, I tore them in pieces; and so within ten days I will do you. Get you to your den again."

All that day Christian and Hopeful lay there, says Bunyan, "in a lamentable case, as before." There seemed no possibility of escape. Then at about midnight "they began to pray, and continued in prayer till almost break of day." A little before then Christian "brake out into this passionate speech: What a fool, quoth he, am I, thus to lie in a stinking dungeon, when I may as well walk in liberty! I have a key in my bosom called Promise that will, I am persuaded, open any lock in Doubting Castle. Then said Hopeful, That's good news, good brother, pluck it out of thy bosom, and try." So he did, and "the door flew open with ease" —then the outward door, and then the iron gate, and they escaped with speed. Awakened by the creaking of the gate, Giant rose to pursue them, but he "felt his limbs to fail, for his fits took him again, so that he could by no means go after them."

You too have a key in your bosom called Promise, for God has given it to you in the Scriptures. Have you ever used it to escape from Doubting Castle? When Satan harasses our conscience and tries to persuade us that there is no forgiveness for such sinners as we are, only a trustful reliance on God's promises to the penitent can liberate us from his harassment. We have to learn in perplexity to rest on the promise of his guidance; in fear, on the promise of his protection; in loneliness, on the promise of his presence. The promises of God, his promises of salvation, can garrison our hearts and minds.

It is in this connection that I think I should refer to the two Gospel sacraments, baptism and the Lord's Supper. Although Protestants have different ways of formulating their understanding of these ordinances, we should be able to accept the dictum from the Second Book of Homilies (1571) that they are "visible signs to which are annexed promises." That the water of baptism and the bread and wine of Communion are "outward and visible signs" is obvious. More particularly, however, they are signs of God's grace, signs which visibly promise his cleansing, forgiveness and new life to those who repent and believe in Jesus. So they elicit and strengthen our faith.

Commandments to Obey

In calling out a people for himself, God told them what kind of people he wanted them to be. They were a special people; he expected from them special conduct. So he gave them the Ten Commandments as a summary of his will, which Jesus underlined in his Sermon on the Mount, uncovering their disturbing implications. The righteousness of his disciples, he said, must exceed the righteousness of the scribes and Pharisees (Mt 5:20). It would be greater in the sense that it would be deeper, a righteousness of the heart, a glad and radical inward obedience.

It is particularly important in our day to emphasize God's call to moral obedience because at least two groups of people are denying it. First, there are the advocates of the so-called New Morality or Situation Ethic, developed in the 1960s. They argue that God's one and only absolute command is love, that all other laws have been abrogated and that love is by itself a sufficient guide to Christian conduct. Whatever is expressive of love is good, they say; whatever is incompatible with it is evil. Now certainly true love, the sacrifice of self in the service of others, is the pre-eminent Christian virtue, and to follow its dictates is extremely demanding. Nevertheless, love needs guidelines, and it is this direction that God's commandments supply. Love does not dispense with law; it fulfills it (Rom 13: 8-10).

Second, there are evangelical Christians who interpret Paul's assertions that "Christ is the end of the law" (Rom 10:4) and that "you are not under law but under grace" (Rom 6:14) as meaning that Christians are no longer under obligation to obey God's moral law. To try to do so, they say, is a legalism which contradicts the freedom Christ has given us. But they misunderstand Paul. The legalism Paul rejected was not obedience to God's law in itself, but the attempt by such obedience to win God's favor and forgiveness. This is impossible, he wrote, for "no human being will be justified in his sight by works of the law" (Rom 3:20).

Once justified by God's sheer grace, however, that is, declared righteous in his sight by his free and un-

deserved favor through Christ, we are then under
obligation to keep his law, and want to do so. Indeed,
Christ died for us precisely "in order that the just re-
quirement of the law might be fulfilled in us" (Rom
8:4), and God puts his Spirit in our hearts in order
to write his law there (Jer 31:33; Ezek 36:27; Gal 5:
22-23). Our Christian freedom, therefore, is freedom
to obey, not to disobey. As Jesus said several times,
if we love him we shall keep his commandments (Jn
14:15, 21-24; 15:14). And it is in Scripture that God's
commandments are to be found.

Thus in the Bible God gives us revelations of himself which lead us to worship, promises of salvation
which stimulate our faith, and commandments ex-
pressing his will which demand our obedience. This is
the meaning of Christian discipleship. Its three essential ingredients are worship, faith and obedience. And
all three are called forth by the Word of God. Worship
is the response to God's self-revelation. It is an adoring
preoccupation with the glory of God, and, as William
Sangster once put it, it can "disinfect us of egoism."
Faith is a restful confidence in the promises of God.
It delivers us from the seesaw of religious experience
—up and down, up and down, Sunday night, Monday
morning. Nothing can deliver us from that but the
promises of God. For our feelings fluctuate, whereas
God's Word remains forever firm. Obedience is a loving commitment to the will of God. It rescues us from
the bog of moral relativism and sets our feet upon
the rock of God's absolute commands.

Moreover, worship, faith and obedience—the three ingredients of discipleship—are all outward looking. In worship we are preoccupied with God's glory, in faith with his promises, in obedience with his commands. Authentic Christian discipleship is never introverted. The Bible is a marvelously liberating book. It pulls us out of ourselves and makes us instead obsessed with God, his glory, promises and will. To love God thus, and to love others for his sake, is to be set free from the tyrannous bondage of our own self-centeredness. The Christian who is engrossed in himself becomes as paralyzed as the self-conscious centipede in the humorous modern parable:

> The centipede was happy quite
> Until a toad in fun
> Exclaimed "which leg comes after which?"
> This put his mind in such a pitch
> He lay distracted in the ditch
> Considering how to run!
>
> While lying in this sorry plight
> A ray of sunshine caught his sight
> And bursting into happy song
> Unthinking he began to run
> And quite forgot the croaker's fun.

Only rays of light from God's Word, which lift our eyes to him, can deliver us from the paralysis which comes from self-preoccupation.

Conclusion

The vital place of the Bible in the Christian life exposes the grave consequences of liberal theology. By undermining public confidence in the reliability of the Bible, it makes Christian discipleship all but impossible. Let me explain. All Christians agree that discipleship includes worship, faith and obedience. They are essential parts of our Christian life. We cannot live as Christians without them. Yet not one of them is possible without a reliable Bible.

How can we worship God if we do not know who he is, what he is like or what kind of worship is pleasing to him? Christians are not Athenians who worship an unknown God. We must know God before we can worship him. And it is the Bible which tells us what he is like.

Again, how can we believe or trust in God if we do not know his promises? Faith is neither a synonym for superstition nor another word for credulity. Faith is a reasoning trust. It rests on the promises of God and on the character of the God who made them. Without promises our faith shrivels up and dies. And God's promises are found in the Bible.

Again, how can we obey God if we do not know his will and commandments? Christian obedience is not blind obedience, but open-eyed and loving. For God has given us commandments in the Bible and shown us that they are not burdensome.

So then, without God's revelation worship is impossible; without God's promises faith is impossible; with-

out God's commandments obedience is impossible.
Without the Bible discipleship is impossible. Do we
realize how blessed we are to have a Bible in our
hands? God has graciously made provision for our
discipleship. He has revealed to us himself, his salvation and his will. He has made it possible for us to worship him, trust him and obey him—in other words, to
live as his loving children in the world.

We need then to come expectantly to the Bible each
day. The great curse of our Bible reading, whenever
it becomes just a stale and boring routine, is that we
do not come to it expectantly. We don't come with confidence that God is willing, able and eager to speak to
us through his Word. We need to come to the Bible
every day with the petition of Samuel on our lips,
"Master, speak; your servant is listening." And he
will! Sometimes through his Word he will give us a
revelation of himself: we shall perceive something of
his glory, our heart will be deeply moved within us,
and we shall fall down and worship him. Sometimes
through his Word he will give us a promise: we shall
grasp it, lay hold of it and say, "Lord, I'm not going to
let it go until I inherit it and until it becomes true of
me." Sometimes through the Bible he will give us a
command: we shall see our need to repent of our disobedience, and we shall pray and resolve that by his
grace we shall obey his command in years to come.

These revelations, promises and commandments
we shall store up in our minds until our Christian
memory becomes like a well-stocked cupboard. From

its shelves in moments of need we shall be able to take down truths or promises or commandments which are appropriate to the situation in which we find ourselves. Without this we condemn ourselves to perpetual immaturity. Only if we meditate on the Word of God, listen to God speaking to us, hear his voice and respond to him in worship, faith and obedience, will we grow into maturity in Christ.

Postscript

I have been concerned in this little book both with the Bible's "yesterday," its historical origins, and its "today," its contemporary relevance. I have tried to develop a simple, Trinitarian doctrine of Scripture as a message which comes from God (he spoke it and speaks it), focuses on Christ (he witnesses to it as witnessing to him) and was articulated by the Holy Spirit through the human authors so that his words and theirs coincided. The practical usefulness of the Bible today, both for the church and for the individual Christian, depends on our acceptance of its divine origin and purpose. Paul combined these things when he described all Scripture as being on the one hand "God-breathed" and on the other "useful" (2 Tim 3:16-17 NIV). It is profitable for us ("for teaching, rebuking, correcting and training in righteousness," NIV) precisely because it was breathed out of the mouth of God. So our view and our use of the Bible go together. It matters what we think about it.

I, for one, am deeply disturbed by the cavalier attitude to the Bible adopted by many, and I long to see it reinstated in the hearts and homes of Christian people and enthroned in the pulpits of the world. Only then can the church again hear and heed God's Word. Only then will God's people learn to integrate their faith and their lives, as they seek to apply the teaching of Scripture to their moral standards, economic lifestyle, marriage and family, work and citizenship. Only then can Christians hope to be the world's salt and light, as Jesus said they were to be, and influence their countries' culture, institutions and laws, values and ideals.

The practical profitability of Scripture for church and Christian, home and nation, should not, however, be our main reason for desiring its reinstatement, but rather the glory of God. If the Bible may rightly be called the Word of God, though spoken through the words of men, then clearly to neglect it is to neglect him, while to listen to it is to listen to him. The overriding reason we should "let the word of Christ dwell in [us] richly" (Col 3:16) is not that we shall thereby be enriched, but that he will thereby be honored and glorified. He wants us to have a Christian mind as well as to live a Christian life. But to have a Christian mind we must have his mind, "the mind of Christ" (compare 1 Cor 2:16 and Phil 2:5). And our minds can be conformed to his mind only as they become soaked in his Word. That is why the Bible is God's book for God's people.

For further reading

Revelation, Inspiration and Authority

Hammond, T. C. *In Understanding Be Men*. Downers Grove, Ill.: InterVarsity Press, 1968. Part I.

Milne, Bruce. *Know the Truth*. Downers Grove, Ill.: InterVarsity Press, 1982. Part I.

Packer, J. I. *Freedom, Authority and Scripture*. London: Inter-Varsity Fellowship, 1982.

Packer, J. I. *God Has Spoken*. Downers Grove, Ill.: InterVarsity Press, 1980.

Understanding the Bible

Balchin, John F. *Understanding Scripture*. Downers Grove, Ill.: InterVarsity Press, 1981.

Bridgland, Cyril. *Pocket Guide to the Old Testament*. London: Inter-Varsity Fellowship, 1982.

Foulkes, Francis. *Pocket Guide to the New Testament*. Downers Grove, Ill.: InterVarsity Press, 1978.

Sterrett, T. Norton. *How to Understand Your Bible*. 2nd ed., rev. Downers Grove, Ill.: InterVarsity Press, 1974.

Stott, John R. W. *Understanding the Bible*. Grand Rapids: Zondervan, 1980.

Studying the Bible

Job, John B., ed. *How to Study the Bible*. Downers Grove, Ill.: InterVarsity Press, 1972.

Lee, P., Scharf, G., and Willcox, R. *Food for Life*. Downers Grove, Ill.: InterVarsity Press, 1977.

Sproul, R. C. *Knowing Scripture*. Downers Grove, Ill.: InterVarsity Press, 1980.

White, John. *The Fight*. Downers Grove, Ill.: InterVarsity Press, 1977. Chapter 3.

65723

N.T. SUMMARY 30 O.T. 17f
DISAGREEMENT 56f
ETERNITY 62
Metaphor 63

220.13
ST 88
c. 1